GOD BLESS OUR TEACHERS

GOD Bless Our Teachers

A TRIBUTE TO TEACHERS

Walter the Educator

SKB

Silent King Books

dedicated to all the teachers across the world

Contents

Why I Created this Book?

Creating a poetry book celebrating teachers is a wonderful way to acknowledge and appreciate the significant impact they have on our lives. Teachers play a vital role in shaping minds, inspiring curiosity, and nurturing the potential within each student. Through poetry, we can capture and express the profound gratitude, respect, and admiration we have for educators. A poetry book dedicated to teachers can serve as a heartfelt tribute, highlighting their dedication, compassion, and unwavering commitment to guiding and empowering future generations. It can also serve as a source of inspiration for both teachers and students, reminding them of the transformative power of education.

One

key holders

In the realm of knowledge, they hold the key,
Guiding minds with wisdom, setting spirits free.
Teachers, the beacons of inspiration,
Igniting flames of curiosity, without hesitation.
    With passion in their souls, they embark,
On a noble journey, leaving an indelible mark.
In classrooms filled with laughter and cheer,
They nurture dreams, year after year.
    They sow the seeds of wisdom and grace,
In every student's heart, a lasting embrace.
Patiently they teach, with unwavering devotion,
Instilling values and stirring emotions.
    They mold the minds of the young and bright,
Illuminating the path, shining a guiding light.
Through their words and actions, they inspire,
Fanning the flames of dreams, higher and higher.

They are the catalysts of change and growth,
Empowering minds, helping them both,
To reach for the stars, to soar and thrive,
With knowledge and skills, they will survive.

From the ABCs to complex equations,
Teachers impart knowledge, sparking elation.
They unlock the doors to endless possibilities,
Empowering minds, shaping destinies.

In the classroom's sacred space,
They create an environment, a special place,
Where curiosity and wonder will forever reside,
And the thirst for knowledge will never subside.

So let us celebrate these guiding stars,
Whose dedication and love will carry us far.
To all the teachers, we raise our voice,
Thank you for giving us the gift of choice.

Two

our eternal debt

In the realm of knowledge, they stand tall,
Guiding us through life's boundless sprawl.
With wisdom's torch, they light the way,
Teachers, the heroes of every day.

They sow the seeds of curiosity,
Nurturing minds with great tenacity.
Patiently they unlock each mind's door,
Inspiring dreams we couldn't see before.

In classrooms filled with laughter and cheer,
They wipe away every trace of fear.
Their words ignite a passion within,
Fueling the fires that lie deep within.

From equations to words that dance and rhyme,
Teachers transform the mundane into sublime.
They sculpt young minds like artists at play,
Molding futures with love every single day.

Beneath their wings, we learn to soar,
In their embrace, we find so much more.
They see our potential when we feel small,
And give us wings to fly, to stand tall.

Through their teachings, we become aware,
Of the wonders that lie beyond compare.
They spark imagination, unleash our might,
Guiding us through darkness into the light.

So let's celebrate these champions of grace,
Whose impact no time can ever erase.
To teachers, we owe our eternal debt,
For their love and knowledge, we'll never forget.

Three

light the way

In the realm of knowledge, they reside,
Guiding us with wisdom, side by side.
Teachers, the architects of our minds,
Unveiling the beauty that learning finds.

Like beacons, they illuminate the way,
Igniting passions that never sway.
Patiently, they unfold each new page,
Filling our hearts with inspiration's gauge.

Their words, like melodies, soothing and clear,
Echoing in our souls, year after year.
With gentle hands, they nurture our dreams,
Fostering growth, like flowing streams.

In classrooms, their magic comes alive,
Creating a space where we all thrive.
They mold young minds with delicate care,
Instilling values, beyond compare.

From history's tales to scientific quests,
They unravel the world, leaving us impressed.
With open hearts, they embrace each child,
Teaching empathy, making spirits wild.

They encourage curiosity's flame,
Teaching us that learning has no shame.
With every lesson, they plant a seed,
Helping us grow, fulfill our every need.

Teachers, the guardians of knowledge's gate,
They shape our futures, our destinies create.
In their hands, lies the power to inspire,
To ignite flames of greatness, to take us higher.

So let us celebrate these heroes in our lives,
Whose dedication and passion never dies.
For they are the ones who light the way,
Guiding us towards a brighter day.

Four

unwavering love

In the realm of knowledge, they stand tall,
Guiding us through life's winding hall.
Teachers, the architects of our minds,
Unveiling wisdom, the rarest finds.

With passion burning in their eyes,
They ignite the spark that never dies.
Patiently they sow seeds of curiosity,
Nurturing minds with boundless generosity.

In classrooms, their magic unfolds,
A symphony of stories yet untold.
They paint pictures with words so fine,
Transporting us to worlds divine.

From math equations to history's lore,
They help us unlock each closed door.
They teach us to think, to analyze,
To question, explore, and empathize.

With hearts that overflow with care,
They mold our dreams with utmost flair.
They shape futures with tender grace,
Empowering us to find our place.

And when the storm clouds gather near,
They wipe away each trembling tear.
Through trials and triumphs, they remain,
A beacon of hope amidst the strain.

So let's celebrate these guiding stars,
Whose impact reaches near and far.
To the teachers, we raise our voice,
For their unwavering love, we rejoice.

Five

unsung heroes

In the realm of knowledge, they stand tall and bright,
Guiding us through darkness, like stars in the night.
Teachers, the keepers of wisdom untold,
Their passion and dedication, worth more than gold.

With patience and care, they ignite our minds,
Nurturing curiosity that forever binds.
They unlock the doors to worlds unseen,
Inspiring dreams and making them gleam.

In classrooms where silence finds its voice,
They teach us to question, to challenge, to rejoice.
With words as their brush, they paint the way,
Creating a masterpiece, day after day.

They mold young minds with compassion and grace,
Shaping futures, leaving an indelible trace.
Their lessons extend beyond books and tests,
Instilling values and fostering success.

Through struggles and triumphs, they never waver,
In their relentless pursuit of knowledge's flavor.
With open hearts, they share their light,
Illuminating paths, making darkness take flight.
So, let us celebrate these beacons of inspiration,
Whose impact on lives surpasses mere admiration.
For teachers, the unsung heroes we adore,
We thank you, today and forevermore.

Six

forever loom

In the realm of knowledge, they reside,
Guiding us with wisdom, side by side.
Teachers, the architects of young minds,
Unveiling worlds, where inspiration binds.

With gentle words and patient grace,
They nurture dreams, igniting the chase.
From letters and numbers to complex theories,
They illuminate paths, dispelling our worries.

In classrooms adorned with dreams untold,
They sculpt futures, creating the bold.
Their passion, like a flame, never fades,
As they empower minds and unveil shades.

They sow the seeds of curiosity,
Fanning the flames of creativity.

Inquiring minds, they help us ignite,
Unleashing imagination's might.

They are the beacons amidst life's storm,
Encouraging dreams to take their form.
With steady hearts and unyielding care,
They shape the leaders of tomorrow's share.

Through laughter, challenges, and tears,
They inspire us to conquer our fears.
In their embrace, knowledge finds a home,
A sanctuary where dreams freely roam.

So let us celebrate the teachers' might,
Their dedication shining ever bright.
For in their hands, a world does bloom,
With gratitude, our hearts shall forever loom.

Seven

shape our legacy

In halls of knowledge, where minds take flight,
There dwells a beacon, a guiding light.
Teachers, those heroes, with wisdom untold,
Their stories of inspiration, forever unfold.

In classrooms they stand, with passion profound,
Nurturing young minds, where possibilities abound.
With patience and care, they ignite the flame,
For knowledge is power, and they play the game.

They sow seeds of wisdom, with words so kind,
Unlocking the treasures within every mind.
They shape the future, with love and grace,
Leaving footprints of knowledge in every space.

They teach us to dream, to reach for the sky,
To never give up, even when dreams seem shy.

They inspire us to learn, to explore and grow,
To embrace the challenges, and let knowledge flow.

Through valleys of doubt, they guide our way,
Encouraging us to persevere, day by day.
They believe in our potential, when we cannot see,
They empower us to be all that we can be.

With words of encouragement, they lift us high,
Helping us spread our wings, ready to fly.
They challenge our minds, and broaden our view,
Teaching us compassion, and empathy too.

In their presence, we find solace and trust,
For they are the pillars, in whom we entrust.
They mold our character, with values so rare,
Their impact on our lives, beyond compare.

So let us celebrate, these guardians of light,
Whose dedication shines through, both day and night.
For they are the architects of our destiny,
The unsung heroes, who shape our legacy.

Eight

as long as we live

From the start of every day,
Teachers guide us on our way.
With patience and with care,
They help us learn and grow and dare.
Through lessons, lectures, and more,
They show us what we can explore.
They teach us skills we'll use for life,
And guide us through the stress and strife.
They work so hard, day and night,
To make sure we're all alright.
They inspire us to be our best,
And help us pass each and every test.
So let's take a moment to say,
Thank you to teachers every day.
For all they do, for all they give,
We owe them thanks as long as we live.

Nine

forever grateful

In classrooms bright, where knowledge gleams,
Where dreams are sparked with guiding beams,
There stands a soul, so wise and true,
A teacher kind, we all look up to.

With patient hearts and nurturing care,
They plant the seeds, so strong and rare,
They shape our minds, unleash our might,
And guide us through the darkest night.

They teach us more than books can hold,
Instilling values, making us bold,
With words of wisdom and gentle sway,
They mold us in their own special way.

From numbers, letters, to tales of old,
They paint the world in stories untold,
They ignite the spark of curiosity,
And foster a love for lifelong learning.

When doubts arise and fears take hold,
They offer solace, like knights of old,
With open arms and steadfast grace,
They help us find our rightful place.

Through laughter, tears, and every test,
They encourage us to do our best,
They see our potential, hidden within,
And push us further, to rise and win.

Oh, teachers dear, we sing your praise,
For all the light you've brought our ways,
In hearts and minds, your legacy stays,
Forever grateful, for all your days.

Ten

more than gold

In halls of knowledge, where wisdom thrives,
There lies a beacon, where greatness arrives.
A teacher's heart, a guiding light,
Ignites the minds, so eager, so bright.

They weave the tapestry of dreams,
With patience, love, and silent screams.
They mold the clay, the young and bold,
Their stories, lessons, never grow old.

With books and words, they open doors,
To vast horizons, uncharted shores.
They fuel the fire of curiosity's flame,
And kindle passion, in every name.

In classrooms filled with laughter's glee,
They plant the seeds of what could be.
They nurture talents, hidden and rare,
And show the world, it's yours to share.

Through struggles faced, they lend a hand,
Giving courage, helping students stand.
They wipe away tears, heal every scar,
Teachers, the unsung heroes they are.

With empathy and understanding true,
They see potential where others see few.
They shape the future, young hearts they mold,
A legacy that shines, worth more than gold.

So raise a toast, let voices ring,
To teachers who make the angels sing.
For their dedication, love, and care,
We celebrate, a debt we share.

For they are the stars that light the way,
Guiding us through each and every day.
Forever grateful, their impact profound,
Teachers, our heroes, forever renowned.

Eleven

treasure untold

In halls of learning, where wisdom thrives,
Resides the power to shape countless lives.
Teachers, the architects of souls,
Unveiling infinite paths to unfold.

With patience as their guiding light,
They spark curiosity, ignite the plight,
Of young minds hungry for knowledge's grace,
In their embrace, dreams find their place.

They're storytellers, weaving tales,
Of heroes, history, and ancient trails.
They paint the canvas of imagination,
Inspiring dreams, sparking creation.

In classrooms filled with laughter's glee,
They nurture minds, setting spirits free.

With words of encouragement, they uplift,
Building confidence, a priceless gift.
    Through every challenge, they stand tall,
Guiding students to conquer all.
They see potential where others may not,
Turning "I can't" into "I will, I've got!"
    With open hearts and minds so bright,
They illuminate darkness, bringing forth light.
They plant seeds of knowledge deep within,
Cultivating minds to bloom and begin.
    From math to art, from science to prose,
They guide us through life's ebbs and flows.
Their passion burns like a blazing fire,
Fueling our dreams to reach higher.
    So let us celebrate these beacons of light,
Who guide us through the darkest night.
Teachers, our heroes, forever we hold,
The wisdom they impart, a treasure untold.

Twelve

wisdom so bright

In halls of wisdom, their spirits reside,
Guiding our minds, with knowledge as their tide.
Teachers, the architects of countless dreams,
Unleashing potential, like sun's golden beams.

With patience as their canvas, they paint a path,
Nurturing minds, igniting a love that'll last.
From the alphabet's embrace to complex equations,
They unravel mysteries, sparking revelations.

In classrooms adorned with stories of old,
They kindle imaginations, worth more than gold.
Through Shakespeare's words and scientific laws,
They foster curiosity, as each mind unfurls.

They listen, they inspire, they lead the way,
Empowering the young to seize each new day.

They're silent heroes, shaping future's might,
Instilling values that make the world ignite.
    With books as allies, they conquer doubt's plight,
Enlightening souls, like stars in the night.
They teach us resilience, to brave life's storms,
Bridging divides, embracing diverse norms.
    From blackboards to screens, their spirit transcends,
Adapting their craft, as technology amends.
In a world ever-changing, they stand steadfast,
Guiding generations, from the present to the past.
    Oh, teachers, we sing your praises so true,
For your unwavering dedication, we honor you.
In the tapestry of life, you're a vibrant thread,
Molding hearts and minds, paving paths ahead.
    So let's celebrate these champions of light,
Who illuminate the world, with wisdom so bright.
Teachers, we thank you, for all that you do,
For shaping our futures, with hearts ever true.

Thirteen

architects of our mind

In halls of knowledge, where wisdom blooms,
There dwell the souls who light up rooms.
With gentle hearts and minds afire,
Teachers inspire, they never tire.

They weave their dreams with lessons bold,
Guiding minds, nurturing hearts untold.
With patient hands and eyes that see,
They shape the future, setting spirits free.

Like artists, they paint the canvas bright,
Igniting sparks, igniting light.
They mold the clay, with love and care,
Creating minds aware, beyond compare.

In classrooms filled with hopes and dreams,
Teachers sow seeds, so it seems.
They cultivate curiosity's might,
Igniting flames of knowledge's light.

They are the beacons, guiding the way,
Through learning's vast and endless bay.
With words they weave, with passion they speak,
Teaching us lessons, both strong and meek.

They are the heroes, unsung and true,
Their dedication, forever in view.
For in the hearts of countless souls,
Their influence forever holds.

So let us honor, with utmost grace,
Teachers who leave an indelible trace.
For they are the architects of our mind,
Whose impact transcends space and time.

Fourteen

the power education

In the realm of knowledge, they reside,
Guiding us on a wondrous ride.
Teachers, the torchbearers of light,
Igniting minds with their insightful might.

They wield words like magic spells,
Unraveling mysteries, casting their spells.
With patience and passion, they impart,
The wisdom that lingers, igniting the heart.

From the blackboard to the digital screen,
They shape dreams, like an artist's scene.
With nurturing hands and caring hearts,
They inspire us to play our parts.

In classrooms filled with laughter and cheer,
They wipe away every trace of fear.

Encouraging us to always strive,
To reach for the stars and truly thrive.

They spark curiosity, like a flame,
Fanning the embers of our inner flame.
Teaching us to question, to explore,
To seek knowledge, forevermore.

In every lecture, every lesson taught,
Their dedication can never be bought.
They open the gates to endless possibilities,
Empowering us with limitless capabilities.

So let us celebrate these beacons of light,
Whose impact shines clear, so bright.
For without them, where would we be?
Lost in a world without knowledge, you see.

Teachers, we salute your unwavering devotion,
For you shape the future with boundless emotion.
In our hearts, your influence remains,
A testament to the power education sustains.

Fifteen

dreams come true

Teachers are the ones who light up our way,
Guiding us through each and every day.
They mold our minds and shape our thoughts,
Empowering us to reach the highest spots.

They are the ones who ignite our curiosity,
And help us to break the bounds of mediocrity.
Their lessons stay with us for a lifetime,
Inspiring us to always strive and climb.

They are the ones who see potential in us,
And push us to achieve with every ounce of trust.
Their wisdom and knowledge we'll carry on,
And make them proud after they're gone.

So let's take a moment to celebrate,
Our teachers who make our lives great.
We thank them for all they do,
And for helping us make our dreams come true.

Sixteen

never be paid

In the classroom, they stand tall
Guiding us through each and every hall
Their wisdom and knowledge, forever will stay
In our hearts and minds, every single day
They teach us to read, write, and spell
And instill in us values that will forever dwell
Their patience and kindness, we can never repay
For they shape our future in every way
From math to science, history to art
They pour their hearts out, playing their part
In shaping the minds of the young and bright
And helping us reach for the highest height
So let us give thanks to our teachers today
For their dedication and hard work, come what may
We owe them a debt that can never be paid
But we can promise to make them proud and never fade.

Seventeen

Teachers, oh Teachers

Teachers, oh Teachers, we praise your noble name
For you carry the torch of knowledge, and light up our flame
You teach us to read, to write, and to grow
To think for ourselves, to ask and to know

Your lessons are more than just books and facts
You guide us through life, and help us to act
With kindness and patience, you lead by example
And show us the way, through the world's ample

Your classrooms are sanctuaries, where we can explore
And discover new things, that we've not seen before
You inspire us to dream, and to aim for the skies
To reach for the stars, and to never compromise

So to all the teachers out there, we thank you from
our hearts
For being our mentors, our guides and our charts

You've made a difference in our lives, and we'll never forget
The lessons you've taught us, and the memories we've met.

Eighteen

molding hearts and minds

In halls of learning, where knowledge intertwines,
There stands a figure, a beacon that shines,
With wisdom and patience, they lead the way,
Guiding young minds to a brighter day.

Teachers, the architects of endless dreams,
Ignite the flame, where curiosity gleams,
They sow the seeds of wisdom, deep and true,
Nurturing potential in everything they do.

In classrooms adorned with colors and art,
They foster growth, igniting a spark,
From numbers to letters, from science to art,
They sculpt young minds, shaping each part.

They listen with care, with open hearts,

Embracing diversity, the many vibrant parts,
Encouraging dreams, they nourish each soul,
Fostering confidence, making each student whole.

With words of encouragement, they uplift,
Instilling resilience, a powerful gift,
They teach not just lessons, but life's profound truths,
Helping students discover their own unique roots.

Through laughter and tears, they stand by our side,
In moments of triumph, and when fears collide,
They believe in our potential, our limitless might,
Guiding us forward, like a guiding light.

So let us celebrate these heroes so dear,
Whose impact on lives is forever clear,
For they shape the future, molding hearts and minds,
Teachers, we salute you, for you are one of a kind.

Nineteen

steadfast love

In halls of wisdom, where knowledge blooms,
Lies the heart of a teacher, shining through.
Guiding minds with patience, their light consumes,
A beacon of inspiration, tried and true.

They ignite the flames within eager hearts,
With words that dance like poetry in the air.
Nurturing dreams, their wisdom imparts,
Empowering souls, with the strength to dare.

From alphabet's embrace to complex theories,
Their passion fuels the quest for understanding.
Through trials and errors, they ease our worries,
With steadfast love, eternally expanding.

They mold our minds like sculptors at their craft,
Unveiling the beauty that lies within.
With gentle hands and lessons that will last,
They shape our futures, where dreams begin.

In every classroom, where dreams take flight,
Teachers weave the tapestry of our lives.
With boundless patience, they illuminate,
The path to knowledge, where greatness thrives.

So let us celebrate these guiding stars,
Whose dedication knows no bounds or ends.
For in their hands, we find who we are,
And in their hearts, our gratitude transcends.

Twenty

passion and dedication

In the realm of knowledge, they reside,
Guiding souls on a wondrous ride.
Teachers, the architects of dreams,
Unleashing potential, like sunbeams.

With open hearts and minds so bright,
They ignite curiosity, shining light.
From ancient lore to future's scope,
They fill young minds with boundless hope.

In classrooms, their magic unfolds,
Stories and lessons, their tales untold.
They paint the canvas of young minds,
With colors of wisdom, the rarest kinds.

They mold the clay of future's seed,
Nurturing growth with every deed.

Patience their virtue, kindness their creed,
They sow the seeds of wisdom indeed.

Through laughter and tears, they stand so tall,
As pillars of strength, inspiring all.
They shape the future, one child at a time,
Teaching compassion, a virtue so prime.

They hold the keys to unlock the door,
To knowledge's vast and endless shore.
With passion and dedication, they impart,
Lessons that linger, etched in the heart.

So let us celebrate these guiding stars,
Whose impact reaches near and far.
For they are the heroes, silent and strong,
Who shape the world, where dreams belong.

igniting minds

In the realm of knowledge, they reside,
Guiding us with passion, far and wide.
Teachers, the architects of our minds,
Unveiling wisdom, the rarest finds.

They sow the seeds of curiosity,
Igniting flames of learning, brilliantly.
With patience and dedication, they teach,
Empowering dreams, within our reach.

In classrooms filled with laughter and cheer,
They inspire us to conquer all our fear.
They nurture talents, like tender shoots,
Molding us into future astute.

Through their words, they shape our destiny,
Unleashing potential, setting us free.

They light the way, when darkness looms,
Leading us towards brighter tombs.
  Their lessons transcend the boundaries of books,
They teach us to question, explore and look.
They are the beacons in our stormy seas,
Teaching us to embrace life's uncertainties.
  With every word, they kindle a spark,
Igniting minds, even in the dark.
Their impact eternal, like a flowing river,
Forever grateful, we shall deliver.
  So let us celebrate these guiding lights,
Who make our future shine so bright.
To teachers, we raise our voice and say,
Thank you for lighting our way, each day.

Twenty-Two

building futures

In the realm of knowledge, they reside,
Guiding minds with wisdom, far and wide.
Teachers, the beacons of light they shine,
Igniting the flame, the love for the divine.
    With passion and patience, they impart,
In classrooms, they etch knowledge in every heart.
Like artists, they paint dreams on the canvas of minds,
Unleashing potential, breaking all the binds.
    They are the architects of a better tomorrow,
Molding characters, erasing sorrow.
In each student's journey, they play their part,
Nurturing brilliance, igniting a spark.
    They unravel mysteries, unlock doors,
Empowering students to explore uncharted shores.

In their words, the universe unfolds,
Inspiring young minds to be bold.

They are heroes, unsung and true,
Building futures, shaping the youth.
Their impact stretches beyond the four walls,
Creating ripples that resonate in all halls.

They embody patience, understanding, and care,
Their lessons, beyond textbooks, they share.
For they know education is not just about facts,
But about molding hearts, nurturing impacts.

So let us raise a toast to these mentors, so great,
Whose dedication and love never abate.
In this ode to teachers, let our voices ring,
Grateful for the knowledge they bring.

Twenty-Three

every single day

Teachers, oh teachers,
The light of our way,
Guiding us through life,
Every single day.

Their wisdom and knowledge,
Is a treasure to keep,
Their patience and kindness,
Make our learning complete.

From math to literature,
They teach us with care,
Preparing us for the future,
And challenges we'll bear.

So let's raise a toast,
To the teachers who inspire,
For their dedication and passion,
We'll always admire.

Twenty-Four

trials and triumphs

In the realm of knowledge, they hold the key,
Guiding minds with wisdom for all to see.
Teachers, the architects of endless dreams,
Unleashing potential, like flowing streams.

With patience and love, they sow the seeds,
Nurturing intellect with compassionate deeds.
Mentors and leaders, they light the way,
Igniting curiosity, day after day.

In classrooms, their passion brightly shines,
Illuminating hearts, like stars align.
They challenge, inspire and help us grow,
Instilling values that forever glow.

In every subject, they share their might,
Unveiling wonders, like a beacon of light.
From numbers to words, from science to art,
Teachers ignite the fire within every heart.

They empower us with knowledge profound,
Encouraging greatness, never to be bound.
Through trials and triumphs, they stand tall,
Building futures, shaping destinies for all.

Their dedication knows no bounds,
Creating a world where potential resounds.
For in the embrace of their loving care,
Lies the power to change, to create, to dare.

So let us honor these champions of the mind,
Whose impact on humanity is one of a kind.
Teachers, the guardians of wisdom and grace,
We celebrate you, your legacy we embrace.

teach and learn

In a realm of knowledge, they reside,
Guiding minds with passion and stride.
Teachers, the beacons of wisdom's light,
Illuminate our paths, day and night.

With patience like a river's flow,
They sow the seeds of knowledge to grow.
Nurturing each tender bud they find,
Unleashing dreams within the mind.

In classrooms adorned with tales untold,
Their words weave wonders, manifold.
They paint the canvas of curiosity,
Igniting flames of possibility.

From math's equations to history's lore,
They unlock the doors of knowledge's store.
With every lesson, they impart,
They shape our souls with tender art.

Through struggles, they lend their guiding hand,
Helping us rise, helping us stand.
They soothe our doubts, calm our fears,
Wiping away our hesitant tears.

They see the potential deep within,
Even when we cannot begin.
They ignite the spark of confidence,
Nurturing dreams with immense reverence.

Teachers, the architects of dreams,
Building bridges where hope gleams.
You sculpt the futures yet to be,
With love and care, we'll always see.

So let us celebrate these noble souls,
Whose impact stretches beyond their roles.
For in their hearts, a flame does burn,
That fuels the desire to teach and learn.

Twenty-Six

gift so pure

In the realm where knowledge blooms,
Through the halls of countless rooms,
There stands a beacon strong and true,
A teacher's heart, forever anew.

They are the guides, the ones who share,
Their wisdom lifts us, everywhere,
In lectures, books, and tales untold,
They shape our minds, make us bold.

With patience, grace, and steady hand,
They help us see, they understand,
They sow the seeds of curiosity,
And nurture dreams with authenticity.

From numbers to words, from science to art,
They ignite the flames within our heart,
They foster growth, ignite the spark,
And light the way, through the dark.

They see the potential, hidden within,
They believe in us, when we begin,
They inspire us to reach the sky,
To spread our wings, to soar up high.

Through challenges and triumphs alike,
They stand by us, with words so wise,
They cheer us on, when we feel weak,
Their faith in us, forever speaks.

So let us celebrate these teachers dear,
Whose impact lingers year after year,
Their dedication, a gift so pure,
In their hands, the future's allure.

For they are the heroes, the guiding light,
Who shape tomorrow, in their might,
Gratitude we hold, forever true,
To teachers, we owe so much to you.

Twenty-Seven

uplift

In halls of wisdom, their presence known,
Guiding hearts with knowledge sown.
Teachers, the stars that light the way,
Their passion aflame, come what may.

They weave tales of wonder and delight,
Ignite minds with dreams taking flight.
From ancient tales to modern lore,
They open windows to worlds galore.

In classrooms filled with curious minds,
They nurture growth, the seeds they find.
With patience and care, they inspire,
Fueling passions that never tire.

They shape the future, one child at a time,
Instilling values that eternally chime.
With words of encouragement, they uplift,
Empowering dreams, a priceless gift.

Through lessons taught and hurdles crossed,
They embrace every child, no matter the cost.
Unseen heroes, their impact profound,
In every student's journey, they're found.

So let us raise a cheer, a heartfelt praise,
For teachers who brighten our darkest days.
Their dedication and love, ever supreme,
A beacon of hope, in a world that may seem.

In gratitude, we honor their noble quest,
For shaping minds and giving their best.
Teachers, the guardians of knowledge's key,
We celebrate you, our guiding decree.

Twenty-Eight

illuminate our days

In the realm of knowledge, where wisdom dwells,
There shines a beacon, a teacher excels.
With patient hearts and minds so bright,
They guide us through darkness, shedding light.

They mold our thoughts and shape our dreams,
Igniting curiosity, unraveling seams.
With words as brushes, they paint our minds,
Filling our souls with colors that bind.

They nurture the seeds of potential within,
Watering minds, cultivating a garden akin.
Each lesson a seed, sown with care,
In fertile minds, they thrive and bear.

Through laughter and tears, they stand so tall,
A fortress of knowledge, for one and all.
Empowering minds, they build bridges anew,
Connecting worlds, bringing dreams into view.

They inspire, they motivate, they ignite,
A passion for learning, burning so bright.
In classrooms, their presence, a beacon of hope,
Guiding us forward, helping us cope.

For every question they patiently answer,
For every doubt they help us conquer,
For the love they sow in hearts so tender,
We celebrate teachers, our eternal defenders.

So let's raise our voices, in gratitude and praise,
For the teachers who illuminate our days.
Their impact boundless, their influence vast,
In our hearts forever, their legacy will last.

Twenty-Nine

words like melodies

In the realm of knowledge, teachers reside,
Guiding us with wisdom, side by side.
They ignite the flame of curiosity,
Nurturing minds with profound generosity.

Their words like melodies, sweet and clear,
Echoing through the corridors, year after year.
They sow the seeds of dreams in fertile minds,
Unleashing potential that forever binds.

With patience and passion, they light the way,
Through the darkest nights, come what may.
They sculpt our thoughts, shaping our souls,
Empowering us to achieve our goals.

Like beacons of hope, they never falter,
Even when the world around may alter.
They mold us into warriors, brave and strong,
Equipping us to face challenges head-on.

Their lessons transcend the boundaries of time,
Inspiring us to reach for the sublime.
In classrooms filled with laughter and cheer,
They instill values that we hold dear.

Beyond textbooks and tests, they teach us much more,
Life lessons that we'll forever adore.
They ignite the spark of lifelong learning,
Fueling our minds, forever yearning.

So let us raise our voices, loud and clear,
To honor the teachers who are always near.
For they are the guardians of knowledge's gate,
Guiding us towards a brighter fate.

In their presence, we find solace and grace,
Forever grateful for their warm embrace.
To teachers, we owe a debt that can't be measured,
For their love and guidance, we'll be forever treasured.

Thirty

limitless height

In halls of wisdom, where knowledge thrives,
Reside the souls who shape young lives.
Teachers, the beacons of endless light,
Guiding us through the darkest night.

With patience and passion, they sow the seed,
Nurturing dreams, fulfilling every need.
They ignite curiosity, spark the flame,
In hearts and minds, they leave their name.

In classrooms, they weave tales untold,
Unveiling mysteries, ancient and bold.
They paint the canvas of our minds,
With colors vibrant, wisdom that binds.

From history's pages to sciences' realm,
They lead us to wisdom's sacred helm.

With open hearts and minds so vast,
They show us how knowledge is amassed.
    They are the architects of futures bright,
Building bridges to limitless height.
They instill values, teach us to strive,
To reach for the stars, to truly thrive.
    Through challenges and triumphs, they stand tall,
Their dedication inspiring us all.
They shape the world, one student at a time,
Leaving footprints, lasting and sublime.
    So, let us celebrate these guiding stars,
Whose impact reaches near and far.
For in their hands, our futures lie,
Teachers, the heroes who never say goodbye.

Thirty-One

fuel aspiration

In a realm where knowledge blooms,
Amidst the classroom's gentle hums,
There stand the heroes, wise and true,
Teachers, guiding lives anew.

    With hearts aflame, they light the way,
Through thick and thin, come what may,
They spark the fire in curious minds,
Planting seeds that transcend time.

    They shape the future, one soul at a time,
Unraveling mysteries, unlocking the prime,
With patience and passion, they impart,
Lessons that forever leave an imprint on the heart.

    They are the architects of dreams,
Building bridges to endless streams,
Their words, like magic, ignite the thrill,
Of chasing dreams with steadfast will.

In their embrace, we find solace and care,
A haven of wisdom, always there,
They nurture and encourage, gently guide,
Transforming doubts into dreams worldwide.

Through countless hours of dedication,
They inspire, they lead, they fuel aspiration,
Their selfless love knows no bounds,
In their presence, greatness resounds.

So let us raise our voices high,
In praise of teachers, standing by,
For they are the ones who mold and shape,
The future's destiny, a world we'll create.

Thirty-Two

lessons that resonate

In a realm where knowledge thrives,
Amidst the rivers that wisdom derives,
There exists a breed of souls so rare,
Who guide us with patience, love, and care.

Teachers, the architects of our minds,
With boundless passion, their purpose shines,
They shape the future, pave the way,
Igniting a flame that will never sway.

With chalk in hand, they paint on walls,
Lessons that resonate in lecture halls,
From alphabets to complex equations,
They nurture dreams and aspirations.

They kindle curiosity's fire,
Fueling minds with a burning desire,
To seek the truth, to question all,
And never let ignorance befall.

They lead us through life's labyrinth,
Instilling values, a moral compass within,
Teaching resilience, compassion, and grace,
Preparing us for the challenges we'll face.

Their patience, unwavering and strong,
Endures the doubts that often prolong,
They believe in our potential, unseen,
And help us realize what we can truly mean.

In each classroom, a world unfolds,
Where imagination takes hold,
They encourage dreams, big and small,
Empowering us to conquer all.

So let us raise our voices high,
In gratitude and heartfelt sigh,
For the teachers who light our way,
Forever grateful, we shall stay.

Thirty-Three

awaken minds

In the realm of knowledge, they stand tall,
Guiding us through learning's endless sprawl.
Teachers, the sculptors of young minds,
Their wisdom and patience forever binds.

With words of wisdom, they ignite a flame,
Fanning the embers of potential, untamed.
They don the cloak of endless inspiration,
Nurturing dreams with dedication and elation.

In the classroom, their presence beams,
A symphony of knowledge, like vivid dreams.
They unravel mysteries, unlock doors,
Planting seeds of curiosity to explore.

They are the architects of futures bright,
Empowering minds to take flight.

Through lessons taught, both big and small,
They build foundations that never fall.
    Their encouragement is a beacon of hope,
Helping us climb the tallest slope.
They instill confidence, remove doubt,
Teaching us what life's truly about.
    With grace and passion, they educate,
In a world where knowledge is innate.
They awaken minds, expand horizons wide,
Aiding us in conquering life's every stride.
    So let us pause and offer our praise,
To teachers who brighten our learning days.
For their tireless efforts, we'll forever be indebted,
To these champions of wisdom, unsung and respected.

Thirty-Four

open doors

In a realm of knowledge, they stand tall,
Guiding minds, inspiring all.
With wisdom deep and hearts so kind,
Teachers shape the futures they find.

They are the stars that light the way,
In classrooms where dreams hold sway.
With patience, grace, and boundless care,
They nurture seeds, so tender and rare.

With chalk in hand and words that flow,
They paint a world no one can know.
Each lesson taught, a gift bestowed,
Their passion for learning clearly showed.

They sow the seeds of curiosity,
Igniting flames of creativity.
They open doors to worlds unseen,
Unleashing minds, so bright and keen.

They teach us not to just exist,
But to embrace life's endless twist.
To question, seek, and never cease,
To learn, to grow, to find our peace.

In their embrace, we find our worth,
They shape our minds, they shape our earth.
So let us raise our voices high,
To honor teachers near and nigh.

For their devotion, love, and care,
For molding hearts beyond compare.
In this ode to teachers, let it be known,
They are the ones who help us to grow.

Thirty-Five

cultivating growth

In a realm of knowledge, where dreams take flight,
There exists a breed, with wisdom shining bright.
Guiding souls through the labyrinth of learning,
Teachers, the beacons, with passion burning.

With patient hearts, their nurturing embrace,
They mold young minds with love and grace.
Igniting sparks within, like stars in the night,
They illuminate paths, igniting the light.

Through valleys of textbooks and mountains of doubt,
Teachers empower, removing the shroud.
They unlock doors to worlds unknown,
Where curiosity thrives and seeds are sown.

In classrooms alive, where laughter resounds,
Ideas take form, as imagination rebounds.
Teachers, the artists, sculptors of dreams,
Unleashing potential, like flowing streams.

They sow seeds of knowledge, deep in our hearts,
Cultivating growth, where greatness imparts.
With every word spoken, every lesson taught,
They inspire, ignite, leaving an indelible thought.

Though time may pass, their impact remains,
Teachers, the architects, shaping our brains.
Weaving the tapestry of futures untold,
They leave footprints, engraved in gold.

So let us celebrate these heroes of might,
Whose dedication shines, like stars at night.
For in the realm of learning, where knowledge ascends,
Teachers are the compass, our eternal friends.

Thirty-Six

like a river

In the realm of knowledge, they do reside,
Guiding us with wisdom, like a gentle tide.
Teachers, the architects of our minds,
Unraveling mysteries, their purpose defined.

With patience and love, they sow the seeds,
Igniting curiosity, tending to our needs.
In classrooms adorned with colors bright,
They paint the canvas of our dreams, day and night.

From alphabets to equations, they impart,
The treasures of learning, a gift from the heart.
They sculpt our thoughts, like skilled artisans,
Shaping the future with their boundless passion.

In their eyes, we see a spark, a flame,
Fueling our aspirations, igniting our aim.
They foster dreams, helping them take flight,
Empowering us to reach for the highest height.

Through words and stories, they captivate,
Opening windows to worlds we contemplate.
They mold our character, virtues they instill,
Teaching us empathy, and the power to fulfill.

With knowledge as their armor, they fight,
Against ignorance, prejudice, and all that's not right.
They stand as beacons, shining bright,
Illuminating the path, dispelling the night.

To those who dedicate their lives to teach,
Our gratitude, like a river, will forever reach.
For you are the torchbearers, the ones who inspire,
In our hearts, your presence shall never tire.

So let us celebrate the teachers, one and all,
For their unwavering commitment, standing tall.
In this ode we offer, let their praises ring,
For they are the heroes who make our hearts sing.

Thirty-Seven

future bright

In the realm of knowledge, they hold the key,
Teachers, the guides who set young minds free.
With wisdom's torch, they light the way,
Guiding us through life, come what may.

In classrooms filled with laughter and cheer,
They nurture dreams, dispel all fear.
With patience and care, they sow the seed,
Inspiring us to learn, to succeed.

They mold our thoughts, our hearts, our souls,
Empowering us to reach our goals.
With passion and dedication, they impart,
Lessons that stay, deep in our heart.

They shape our minds, ignite curiosity's flame,
Teaching us to question, explore, and frame.
Through trials and triumphs, they stand tall,
Helping us rise, whenever we fall.

With a gentle hand and words of grace,
They uplift, inspire, in every embrace.
Their love for learning, an eternal fire,
Ignites within us, a burning desire.

So here's to the teachers, our cherished guides,
Who illuminate the path where knowledge resides.
In classrooms adorned with hope and light,
They lead us towards a future bright.

About the Author

Walter the Educator is one of the pseudonyms for Walter Anderson. Formally educated in Chemistry, Business, and Education, he is an educator, an author, a diverse entrepreneur, and the son of a disabled war veteran. "Walter the Educator" shares his time between educating and creating. He holds interests and owns several creative projects that entertain, enlighten, enhance, and educate, hoping to inspire and motivate you.

Follow, find new works, and stay up to date with
Walter the Educator™
at www.WaltertheEducator.com